REMEMBER TO DRINK RESPONSIBLY

© Philippe Dufrenoy

© Editions d'Art Class
160, cours du Médoc
33300 Bordeaux • France

Editor : Claude Lada
Interviews in french : Alain Labatut
Translations : Alexandre Rychlewski

© CLASS 2002

PRINTED IN FRANCE

Portraits

en Grands Crus

The city of Bordeaux can boast of a long tradition of commerce thanks to its port, as well as an outstanding architectural heritage. Bordeaux has its own special way of embodying both the past and the future. The city is a centre for the aerospace industry and various high-tech fields, and has one of France's leading universities. Bordeaux's international reputation is nevertheless due to a great extent to the wine that bears its name.

The Bordeaux vineyards reflect the tremendous variety of the surrounding region. The unique soil and human expertise combine to make a product of great finesse. Turned towards the Atlantic, but protected from prevailing winds by the Landes forest, the Bordeaux area has an intrinsic potential to produce very great wines. A subtle blend of several grape varieties offers an infinity of flavors from among the dry white, sweet white, rosé, and red wines of Bordeaux. There is something to satisfy absolutely everybody.

As we all know, wine is a precious addition to any celebration. This is why the city of Bordeaux created a major biennial event, La Fête du Vin. I cordially invite you to participate in the third such Fête, in June 2004.

Acclaimed by wine and spirits professionals from around the world, Bordeaux's VINEXPO has become that sector's leading trade fair, with some 2,500 exhibitors. VINEXPO has been temporarily exported to New York this year, and I wish this exhibition as much success as the prestigious parent event here in Bordeaux.

I now invite you to appreciate the unusual and altogether surprising talent of the Bordeaux painter, Philippe Dufrenoy, who has dipped his brush into wine! His portraits, painted uniquely with great wine, are a highly original way of merging the complementary worlds of art and wine. I very much hope you enjoy "tasting" his work!

Alain JUPPE

Mayor of Bordeaux, Member of the French Parliament, and former Prime Minister of France

W ho would have thought that this divine nectar would ever be used to paint portraits?

One day, after a meal with a friend, intuitively, without really thinking about it, Philippe Dufrenoy took a brush he had kept in his shirt pocket, dipped it into a glass of wine, and started to paint a portrait of his dinner companion on a white paper table-cloth in an inexpensive restaurant.

This sudden inspiration soon took on momentum. The above painting, over time, led to a new artistic technique, and Philippe Dufrenoy's "watercolors" done with wine have culminated in the portrait gallery reproduced in this book. A new kind of paint, taking its colour from tannin and anthocyanins, has become a fitting medium to represent some of the most influential people in the world of Bordeaux wine.

Reflecting our own mortality, these paintings do not last eternally... The wine used in the original paintings has since faded to the point of practically disappearing. However, these portraits were photographed shortly after completion.
They have a natural and uncanny way of capturing the spirit of men and women responsible for making a unique product which provides great joy around the world.

All of the men and women in this book accomplish their work with love and devotion. Having been blessed with a natural gift, neither artist Philippe Dufrenoy nor the people he has painted have left anything else to chance.

Everyone in this book is passionately committed to, and takes joy in, what they do. The fact that these unique paintings are monochrome does not at all detract from the warmth of the smiles.

The portraits have a serenity that inspires confidence. The monochrome presentation also does much to emphasize elegant architectural details.

Wine has finally been used as a means to portray the people who make it, in a highly original fusion that sheds a new light on the wonderful universe of Bordeaux.

The Editor

Summary

Rive droite

CHATEAU CANON Premier Grand Cru Classé

CHATEAU PAVIE Premier Grand Cru Classé

CHATEAU FONROQUE Grand Cru Classé

CHATEAU LA COUSPAUDE Grand Cru Classé

CHATEAU PAVIE DECESSE Grand Cru Classé

CHATEAU RIPEAU Grand Cru Classé

AURELIUS Grand Cru

LE FER Grand Cru

CHATEAU MONBOUSQUET Grand Cru

CHATEAU PAVIE MACQUIN Grand Cru

SANCTUS Grand Cru

CHATEAU TRIMOULET Grand Cru

CHATEAU LA CABANNE Pomerol

CHATEAU MAZEYRES Pomerol

Rive gauche

CHATEAU CARBONNIEUX Grand Cru Classé

CHATEAU MALARTIC LAGRAVIERE Grand Cru Classé

CHATEAU SMITH HAUT LAFITTE Grand Cru Classé

CHATEAU RAUZAN-SEGLA Grand Cru Classé

CHATEAU LEOVILLE BARTON Grand Cru Classé

CHATEAU LANGOA BARTON Grand Cru Classé

CHATEAU CAMENSAC Grand Cru Classé

CHATEAU MONTROSE Grand Cru Classé

CHATEAU LA TOUR CARNET Grand Cru Classé

CHATEAU D'AGASSAC Cru Bourgeois Haut-Médoc

CHATEAU FONBADET Pauillac

CHATEAU LOUDENNE Cru Bourgeois Médoc

CHATEAU SAINT-AHON Cru Bourgeois Haut-Médoc

CHATEAU SIRAN Margaux

Rive droite

John Kolasa

CHATEAU CANON
PREMIER GRAND CRU CLASSE

"At a famous wine estate like Château Canon, one has, perhaps more than elsewhere, the impression of being entrusted with a temporary stewardship… In order to put things into perspective, it is interesting to taste wines produced by preceding generations – a bit like meeting one's children after a long absence… I know for a fact that I will never see the full effects of the investments currently being made at Canon. But the idea of being part of the history of a château as great as this, however briefly, is extremely stimulating."

Château Canon

1ᵉʳ Grand Cru Classé

2000

Saint-Émilion Grand Cru

APPELLATION ST-ÉMILION GRAND CRU CONTRÔLÉE

MIS EN BOUTEILLE AU CHÂTEAU
CHÂTEAU CANON - PROPRIÉTAIRE À SAINT-ÉMILION - FRANCE
PRODUCE OF FRANCE - BORDEAUX

13,5 % vol.   750 ml

Gérard Perse

CHATEAU PAVIE
PREMIER GRAND CRU CLASSE

"Obtaining a ripe crop calls for sacrificing a large part of the yield. Thanks to yields of just 28/30 hectoliters, we are almost sure, even in years like 1998 and 1999 with very rainy autumns, to harvest ripe, healthy grapes. There are, of course, still differences in vintage quality. Our biggest challenge is to make excellent wine in a year where the weather has not been good. This is what we set out to do with Michel Rolland and Laurent Lusseau."

G. PERSE

CHATEAU FONROQUE
GRAND CRU CLASSE SAINT-EMILION

"The changes at Château Fonroque can hardly be termed revolutionary to the extent that nothing really earthshaking is taking place. I prefer to see them rather as a restructuring, involving well thought-out, far-reaching changes...

In the long run, our quality-oriented management and the huge amount of meticulous work we have carried out at Château Fonroque will bring the vineyard into perfect harmony with its environment. Thanks to contact with a living subsoil, without excessive root stress due to the presence of limestone, vines here have a natural tendency to concentrate their vigor on producing grapes with a marked personality, subtlety, and rich complexity – ideal for a genuine vin de terroir... "

Alain Moueix

GRAND CRU CLASSE

CHATEAU
FONROQUE

SAINT-EMILION GRAND CRU
APPELLATION SAINT-EMILION GRAND CRU CONTROLEE

CHATEAU LA COUSPAUDE
GRAND CRU CLASSE SAINT-EMILION

"Our limestone soil has a natural propensity to produce full-bodied, powerful wines with plenty of tannin. However, by closely monitoring ripening and fine-tuning extraction, we also do our best to bring out our terroir's natural finesse… Balance is the byword at La Couspaude, and it is impossible to make the same wine from one year to the next… Above and beyond the right terroir, it takes two good centuries to be able to make a great wine. And what works at La Couspaude won't anywhere else. Unless you aim for a bland, standardized product, the way wine is made on a small quality-oriented estate cannot be reproduced anywhere else."

Jean-Claude Aubert

CHATEAU PAVIE DECESSE
GRAND CRU CLASSE SAINT-EMILION

"The history of Pavie Decesse is inseparable from that of Pavie, whose origins go back at least as far as the 4th century AD. Château Pavie Decesse was part of Pavie until the late 19th century, at which time it became an autonomous estate. Be this as it may, both vineyards have always been considered separate entities, with their own specific terroir. The newly-configured Pavie Decesse is located entirely on the Saint-Emilion limestone plateau where Merlot produces outstanding wines… It would undoubtedly be a mistake to apply the same winegrowing approach at both estates, which was often the case in the past when Pavie Decesse was an enclave of Pavie."

Laurent Lusseau, estate manager

Françoise de Wilde

CHATEAU RIPEAU
GRAND CRU CLASSE SAINT-EMILION

"The long-term efforts to renovate the estate have been going on since 1976. It was important to continue the work already started by my family. I feel a strong emotional commitment to perpetuate what they have done, and am aware that my stewardship of this outstanding estate is only temporary. I am grateful for this opportunity and respect the trust that has been placed in me… Ripeau has slightly gravelly soil and a continuation of the clay-iron vein that runs through Cheval-Blanc and Figeac. I look for the best possible balance every year, making full use of this precious terroir the Good Lord has given me…

I am happy not only to be a woman and a mother, but also to give birth to a new wine, remarkable in its own unique way, every year."

2000

Château Ripeau

GRAND CRU CLASSÉ

SAINT-ÉMILION GRAND CRU
APPELLATION SAINT-ÉMILION GRAND CRU CONTRÔLÉE

G F A DU CHÂTEAU RIPEAU - PROPRIÉTAIRE

S.C.E.A Château Ripeau - Françoise de WILDE A SAINT-ÉMILION - GIRONDE - FRANCE

Alain Naulet

AURELIUS
SAINT-EMILION GRAND CRU

"I can say without any false modesty that the Union de Producteurs is often ahead of the field... We showed the way by adopting the advanced winemaking techniques that have since become a benchmark for quality in Bordeaux. This emphasis on quality is undoubtedly a common thread throughout all the wines produced by the Union. It is also fair to say that we have incredible leeway in selecting and blending our wines due to the wide diversity of our member winegrowers and their fabulous terroirs..."

AURELIUS

2000

Saint-Émilion Grand Cru

Franck Mähler-Besse

LE FER
SAINT-EMILION GRAND CRU

"As traditional négociants, we choose the best wines of Bordeaux and age them in our cellars before shipping them. Today's consumers are looking for the finest quality – top-end wines, as well as great growths either sold on a futures basis or aged in our cellars. We have also invested in quality terroirs in several Bordeaux appellations. Le Fer is the perfect illustration of this. It sums up all that is so special about Saint-Emilion... As producers in our own right, we take great pains to make the very most of our estates, including cuvées that can hold their own with the very best of Bordeaux."

LE FER

2000

SAINT-ÉMILION GRAND CRU

APPELLATION SAINT-ÉMILION GRAND CRU CONTRÔLÉE

MIS EN BOUTEILLE À LA PROPRIÉTÉ

PAR E.U.R.L. CHÂTEAU CHEVAL NOIR

PROPRIÉTAIRE À SAINT-ÉMILION

12,5% vol.   750 ml

PRODUCE OF FRANCE

Gérard Perse

CHATEAU MONBOUSQUET
SAINT-EMILION GRAND CRU

"I bought Monbousquet because of the intense emotion I felt when I first visited the area in 1993. At the time, it wasn't so much a question of terroir – even though the soil at Monbousquet is excellent – but rather the fact that I fell head-over-heels in love with the estate. On the other hand, my decision to buy Pavie and Pavie-Decesse in 1998 was very carefully considered.

It was based largely on technical criteria, and the quality of the terroir was decisive…"

G. PERSE

CHATEAU PAVIE MACQUIN
SAINT-EMILION GRAND CRU

"Paradoxically, until very recently, Pavie Macquin's incredible potential was far from being realized. Located on the limestone plateau of the famous Côte de Pavie, the vines grow on strong clay soil that naturally produces wines with impressive structure and a certain firmness. It is tempting to take the easy road with such a natural inclination, and produce high yields of rather rustic wine. Instead, we make sure to achieve ideal ripeness, low yields, and controlled extraction to show that Pavie Macquin's terroir is capable of producing an outstanding wine – both virile and elegant, as well as very fresh, with an extremely delicate tannic structure…"

Nicolas Thienpont

SANCTUS
SAINT-EMILION GRAND CRU

When we baptized our micro-cuvée "Sanctus", Aurélio Montes and I were aware that we were duty-bound to produce a truly excellent wine.

So, we selected the two best plots at Château La Bienfaisance that regularly produce powerful, elegant wines in order to make a concentrated, outstanding Saint-Emilion… We treat our wine like a work of art, with equal doses of inspiration and rigor. No detail is too unimportant. We look for optimum balance and flavor that will do honor to the superb terroir where the grapes are grown…"

Patrick Baseden

Michel & Joëlle Jean

CHATEAU TRIMOULET
SAINT-EMILION GRAND CRU

"I believe that the continuity of a great wine estate depends on three main things: family, terroir, and tradition. Trimoulet is first and foremost a home for my family… It is also a great terroir, although somewhat difficult to cultivate, calling for very specific viticultural practices.

However, the terroir is remarkably conducive to making great wine… I do my best to make a vin plaisir, an enjoyable, seductive, completely natural wine, in keeping with my terroir.

I am not interested in trends that produce flashy, standardized wines…

At Trimoulet, we refuse to compromise our culture and traditions.

We have a long-term perspective and try not to force anything on nature…"

PRODUCE OF FRANCE

CHATEAU TRIMOULET

SAINT-ÉMILION GRAND CRU

APPELLATION SAINT-ÉMILION GRAND CRU CONTRÔLÉE

MICHEL JEAN
PROPRIÉTAIRE A SAINT-ÉMILION (GIRONDE)
FRANCE

12%Vol.   75cl e

MIS EN BOUTEILLE AU CHATEAU

CHATEAU LA CABANNE
POMEROL

"My husband, Jean-Pierre, had an absolute passion for making fine wine and we always did our utmost to maintain and develop very high standards in all our vineyards… Despite the immense vacuum left by his loss, I am totally committed to continuing the effort with my two children, Marie-Pierre and François. Our primary concern will always be to reflect all that is good in our terroirs, and to give our wines "red-carpet" treatment. Our winegrowing methods combine time-honored know-how with the most up-to-date techniques"

Jean-Pierre Estager

GRAND VIN DE BORDEAUX

CHATEAU LA CABANNE®

POMEROL

APPELLATION POMEROL CONTRÔLÉE

2000

VIGNOBLES J.P. ESTAGER, PROPRIÉTAIRE A POMEROL (GIRONDE) FRANCE

PRODUIT DE FRANCE   PRODUCE OF FRANCE

13,5%alc./vol.   MIS EN BOUTEILLE AU CHÂTEAU   750 ml

Alain Moueix

CHATEAU MAZEYRES
POMEROL

"Making the most of diverse soil types is the keystone of the new winegrowing philosophy at Château Mazeyres. The many-faceted terroir, whose component parts have been studied in depth, enables us to make just the type of wine we desire… Mazeyres produces intrinsically elegant wines… I look for roundness, length, and above all, a creamy, velvety texture in a Pomerol. I strive to make vins de plaisir – enjoyable, seductive wines – that are well-balanced, with lots of charm. Fortunately, this is entirely possible thanks to our fine terroir, our Merlot vines – which make early-maturing wine – and the important complementary role of Cabernet Franc. Château, Mazeyres has good length and complexity… It is currently proving beyond the shadow of a doubt that the estate can produce vins de plaisir in the tradition of the greatest Pomerol estates".

Rive gauche

Antony Perrin

CHATEAU CARBONNIEUX
GRAND CRU CLASSE PESSAC-LEOGNAN

"Our quest for quality calls for never-ending research and experimentation. The large size of Château Carbonnieux's vineyards and the variety of soils gives us ample opportunity… We constantly fine-tune our winegrowing methods, never losing sight of the fact that progress is best achieved by patiently making well thought-out and carefully-tested innovations. These enable us to improve the balance in the vineyard and make the most of our terroir… which we aim to reflect in each and every vintage."

CHÂTEAU CARBONNIEUX
1993
GRAND CRU CLASSÉ DE GRAVES

PES
APPELLATIO

MIS EN BOUTEILL

Sociét
125 % vol.   PROPRIÉTAIRE

GRAND CRU CLASSÉ

1988
CHÂTEAU CARBONNIEUX
PESSAC-LÉOGNAN
APPELLATION PESSAC-LÉOGNAN CONTROLÉE
GRAND VIN DE GRAVES
PRODUCE OF FRANCE
MIS EN BOUTEILLES   AU CHATEAU
12,5 % vol.   Société des Grandes Prayes   75 cl
PROPRIÉTAIRE A LEOGNAN (GIRONDE) FRANCE

CHATEAU MALARTIC-LAGRAVIERE
GRAND CRU CLASSE PESSAC-LEOGNAN

"Wine is, above all, about history. But it is also about life – a series of new beginnings, a never-ending learning experience. When you devote a great deal of time and effort to a unique, inimitable microcosm called a terroir, a love story inevitably develops, a sort of intimate relationship with something that's very much alive. This is the best way I can describe our passion for Malartic-Lagravière… We want to lay the groundwork for something long-lasting. We are extremely attentive to the demands of an extraordinarily complex wine, and have enormous respect for this immense terroir and its long history…"

Alfred-Alexandre & Michèle Bonnie

Daniel Cathiard

CHATEAU SMITH HAUT LAFITTE
GRAND CRU CLASSE PESSAC LEOGNAN

"When blessed with a terroir as outstanding and unique as Smith Haut Lafitte's, it is vital to respect its natural equilibrium. Doing otherwise would surely detract from the wine. This entails paying close attention to the soil – its various layers, the life within it, and the balance between it and the vines – which is the basis for obtaining the best possible fruit. That is the number one priority at Smith Haut Lafitte, where the vines are pampered in an infinite number of ways. This labor-intensive work is comparable to looking after a carefully manicured garden. Furthermore, we are very aware of ecological issues, implementing entirely natural solutions whenever possible. We accept the constraints inherent to making a luxury product.

With this as the starting point, the rest is easy…"

Daniel Cathiard

John Kolasa

CHATEAU RAUZAN-SEGLA
GRAND CRU CLASSE EN 1855

"Humility is definitely in order when dealing with a Terroir as fine and complex as Rauzan-Ségla. My work consists in trying to reflect the unique qualities of this special vineyard.

In doing so, I follow in the footsteps of Pierre des Mesures de Rauzan.

This discoverer of great Terroirs showed how much of a prophet he was when he bought the estate in 1661…

It's only by seeing things in this light that the tradition of excellence that has always reigned at Rauzan-Ségla can be maintained."

GRAND CRU CLASSÉ

Château

RAUZAN-SÉGLA

MARGAUX

APPELLATION MARGAUX CONTRÔLÉE

2000

CHATEAU RAUZAN - SÉGLA - PROPRIÉTAIRE A MARGAUX - FRANCE

13 % vol.   MIS EN BOUTEILLE AU CHATEAU   750 ml

PRODUCT OF FRANCE-BORDEAUX

Anthony Barton

CHATEAU LEOVILLE BARTON
GRAND CRU CLASSE EN 1855

"Léoville Barton's terroir produces wines with a remarkable, unique personality –
a special kind of elegance and subtlety… Those who deny the importance of terroir
are wrong… All you have to do is compare the wines of Léoville and Langoa Barton.
Both vineyards are in the heart of the Saint-Julien appellation, have the same blend
of grape varieties, and are produced the same way. And yet, the two wines are appre-
ciably different…"

CHÂTEAU
LÉOVILLE BARTON
1995
CRU CLASSÉ EN 1855

12,5 % vol.   SAINT-JULIEN   750 ml
APPELLATION SAINT-JULIEN CONTRÔLÉE

S.A. DES CHATEAUX LANGOA ET LÉOVILLE-BARTON
A SAINT-JULIEN-BEYCHEVELLE GIRONDE

MIS EN BOUTEILLE AU CHATEAU

CHATEAU LANGOA BARTON
GRAND CRU CLASSE EN 1855

"I like subtle wines that give food for thought... We are fortunate in Saint-Julien – our wines have a natural tendency towards finesse. This must be preserved at all costs, and not overshadowed by superfluous overextraction...

I do not by any means seek to make hugely concentrated wines...

At Léoville and Langoa Barton, extraction is adapted to the characteristics of each vintage."

Lilian Barton

Lilian Barton

FIDE · ET · FORTITUDINE.

CRU CLASSÉ EN 1855

1998
CHATEAU
LANGOA BARTON
SAINT-JULIEN
APPELLATION SAINT-JULIEN CONTRÔLÉE

S.A. DES CHATEAUX LANGOA ET LEOVILLE-BARTON
A SAINT-JULIEN-BEYCHEVELLE – GIRONDE

MIS EN BOUTEILLE AU CHATEAU
GRAND VIN DE BORDEAUX
12,5% vol.   750 ml

CHATEAU CAMENSAC
GRAND CRU CLASSE EN 1855

"Even a cursory look at the statistics shows that international competition has become very stiff. This makes quality an absolute necessity. At Camensac, our outstanding terroir has been producing classically excellent wine in the finest Médoc tradition for centuries.

Quality at Camensac also means incorporating state-of-the-art techniques, as long as they do not alter the estate's intrinsic characteristics. Technology can be applied anywhere, but a great terroir cannot be invented. It just is… We will never abandon this philosophy in response to trends. We would consider this selling out…"

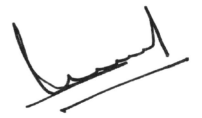

Elisée Forner

Jean-Louis & Anne-Marie Charmolüe

CHATEAU MONTROSE
GRAND CRU CLASSE EN 1855

"Montrose's large vineyard, divided into well-defined plots, and the estate's various buildings are a sort of microcosm of Médoc history… Like my ancestors, I do everything in my power to make best use of this splendid terroir and its fabulous old vines. These are tended in the traditional way, to make a wine that is intrinsically great, and not artificial in any way — the way I love wine. Progress in viticulture and winemaking is quite precious, but it must never take away from a wine's true character. The ultimate factor must be the terroir…"

GRAND CRU CLASSÉ DU MÉDOC EN 1855

Château Montrose

2000

J. L. Charmolüe

CHATEAU LA TOUR CARNET
GRAND CRU CLASSE EN 1855

"Personally, I look at the vineyard's potential when I buy an estate, rather than taking over a property that is already producing at its peak.

I saw the purchase of La Tour Carnet as a major challenge. The rather cool microclimate, the predominately clay-limestone soil, and the recent reconstitution of the original vineyard are all part of the challenge intrinsic to my quest for quality at La Tour Carnet. Our policy of plot by plot vineyard management, the introduction of state-of-the-art methods in the vines and cellars, in short, taking the estate's every particularity into account, has enabled us to make the very most of this fine terroir. The world of wine has acknowledged the improvements at La Tour Carnet which, I am convinced, have only just begun…"

Bernard Magrez

GRAND CRU CLASSÉ DU MÉDOC EN 1855

LA TOUR A ÉTÉ ÉDIFIÉE EN 1120

CHATEAU
LA TOUR CARNET

HAUT-MÉDOC
APPELLATION HAUT-MÉDOC CONTRÔLÉE

1999

Grand Vin de Bordeaux
PRODUCT OF FRANCE

12,5 % vol.   75 cl

BERNARD MAGREZ PROPRIÉTAIRE À ST-LAURENT-DE-MÉDOC

MIS EN BOUTEILLES AU CHATEAU

Jean-Luc Zell

CHATEAU d'AGASSAC
CRU BOURGEOIS HAUT-MEDOC

"Château d'Agassac's two great assets are the quality of its terroir and its old vines – an average of 35 years old. Agassac's terroir has excellent sun exposure and warm, well-drained deep gravel soil. Both of these characteristics account for the fact that grapes ripen very early here… We aim to achieve the highest possible potential from this unique terroir rather than just a simple "product" made thanks to modern technology – even if research can admittedly result in helpful technological advances. Our current efforts are in keeping with Agassac's character, which was plain to see in a mammoth vertical tasting of pre-1996 vintages we organized… Of course, vintages vary because of the weather or the winegrower's touch. What unites them though, is the terroir."

CRU BOURGEOIS

Mis en bouteille
au Château

2000

CHÂTEAU D'AGASSAC

HAUT-MÉDOC

Appellation Haut-Médoc Contrôlée

S.C.A. Château d'Agassac - Propriétaire
A Ludon - Médoc - France
Produit de France

75cl   13% vol

CHATEAU FONBADET
PAUILLAC

"Bordering on Pauillac's most prestigious estates, with three separate parts that have been planted with vines for over three centuries, Fonbadet is perfectly representative of its appellation. And this quintessential Pauillac character is what I wish to maintain more than anything else... Pauillac is justifiably famous for its aging potential. As for myself, my upbringing and personal taste lead me to prefer subtle wines. I appreciate wines that invite discovery and take some coaxing before unveiling their charms...

Other than Fonbadet's considerable aging potential, it is also a priority for me to reflect the other main quality conferred by its terroir: a unique kind of delicate, velvety fruitiness."

Pierre Peyronie and his daughter Pascale

GRAND VIN DE BORDEAUX

Château Fonbadet

PAUILLAC

APPELLATION PAUILLAC CONTRÔLÉE

1999

s.c.e.a. **DOMAINES PEYRONIE**

A PAUILLAC MÉDOC - FRANCE

MIS EN BOUTEILLE AU CHATEAU

12.5% alc. (by vol.)   750 ml

PRODUCE OF FRANCE

Jean-Paul Lafragette

CHATEAU LOUDENNE
CRU BOURGEOIS HAUT-MEDOC

"For me, wine is a lifestyle, a form of esthetics. It is also a passion, even though almost anything seems simpler than making fine wine… The terroir's role can hardly be overestimated, but the tailor-made, craftsmanship aspect of winegrowing is no less important. It is quite heady to be totally responsible for any number of important choices and to integrate all the variables …

Bordeaux can be proud of its enormous range of wines. This complexity is compounded by vintage variations - sometimes subtle, sometimes more marked. Château Loudenne is a fantastic estate, and I am doing all I can to improve quality there even further. Some of these efforts concern infinitesimal details, but they all add up, and I never lose sight of the fact that there is always room for improvement."

CRU BOURGEOIS

CHÂTEAU
Loudenne
MÉDOC
Appellation Médoc Contrôlée

2000

Domaines Lafragette Propriétaire
SCS Château Loudenne Récoltant
Saint-Yzans-de-Médoc 33340 France

MIS EN BOUTEILLES AU CHÂTEAU

750ml e   Produce of France   13% vol.

Comte Bernard de Colbert

CHATEAU SAINT-AHON
CRU BOURGEOIS HAUT-MEDOC

"In my opinion, wine quality depends above all on balance. A great terroir is a fragile microcosm whose equilibrium depends to a large extent on the soil, which must be preserved at all costs. If this is not done, the wine will gradually lose its personality. Obviously, winemaking know-how also has an essential role to play. Winegrowers are constantly faced with a series of choices, and must make the most intelligent ones in order to reflect the terroir's intrinsic balance. Keeping a very close eye on the vines is another major factor in quality. That is because there is no catch-all, simplified way of growing wine grapes. This is especially true when it comes to low yields or how to prune.

The wrong decision can take away from a wine's character and have negative economic ramifications. In short, I look for balance in all respects at Saint-Ahon."

CHATEAU SIRAN
MARGAUX

"Our family has owned Siran for 150 years… So, my time here is very much a continuation of the estate's history as well as paving the way for the future. Above and beyond my ongoing commitment to make the most of the terroir, I am very attached to the heritage that has been passed on by our ancestors. When the time comes, I want to hand over an estate in the best possible condition to my son. I am constantly looking to improve Siran in every way, and make it more attractive…. This obviously concerns the vines and the wine, but also the château, promises and gardens, which I consider a sort of showcase. All aspects of quality count at an estate with a reputation as fine as Siran's…"

Brigitte Miailhe

La cuvée de mon château

2000 2000 2000

CHATEAU SIRAN

MARGAUX

APPELLATION MARGAUX CONTRÔLÉE

SOCIÉTÉ CIVILE DU CHÂTEAU SIRAN
LABARDE · 33460 · FRANCE
Ancienne propriété des comtes de Toulouse Lautrec

13% ALC. by vol   PRODUCT OF FRANCE   150 cl

MIS EN BOUTEILLE AU CHATEAU